# ALL
# POINTS
# BULLETIN

Poems by Sharon Scholl

CLOSET BOOKS and the book colophon are trademarks of The Robert Crane Corporation.


Cover Design by Oscar Senn



1st Edition
First Printing
January 2004

ISBN 1-891232-17-7

Published by
Closet Books
PO Box 440504
Jacksonville, FL 32222

Printed in the United States of America

# TABLE OF CONTENTS

# INTRODUCTION

*"Love calls us to the things of this world."*
Richard Wilbur

The poems in this volume originated from my love of being in new places, venturing out, and coming home a stranger to all I knew before the journey.

Each poem is a probe, a quest for the meaning of a place created for readers who enjoy imaginative journeys. They constitute a travel diary of thirty wandering years, my literary tourist photographs.

The book owes a large debt of gratitude to the publisher of Closet Books, George Gilpatrick and senior editor, Lynn Skapyak Harlin, for their faith in the work and meticulous attention to detail.

The project itself was made possible through a grant from The Community Foundation of Jacksonville, Florida, which is a valuable resource supporting and encouraging community arts in Jacksonville.

# Wanderlust

# Voyage

We stand enchanted at the rail,
figures in relief, cut fragments
in the art of cloud and sail.

Distant lights flicker and fail
through the waves' white ornaments.
We stand enchanted at the rail.

Starlight leaves its glittering trail
on gravity's bent bridge, and hence
in the art of cloud and sail.

Our tall ship sprays a forked tail
of drifting liquid paraments.
We stand enchanted at the rail.

We tip and rise; the sky grows pale
to match the sea, blue complements
in the art of cloud and sail.

The sun is smothered, gray as shale,
by misty vapors low and dense.
We stand enchanted at the rail
in the art of cloud and sail.

## ms Statendam

Brown man, brown suit:
buckets, mops,
waiters' trays,
brass polish cloths,
trash cans,
ironing boards,
vacuum sweepers,
luggage racks,
mooring lines,
scars.

White man, white suit:
calculators, voice mail,
computer terminal,
chef's hat,
ship's radio,
global positioning system,
engines, ship's log,
public address system,
awards.

This is the world they made when
the brown and the white man met.

# NETHERLANDS

## Amsterdam Houseboats

They only meant to fish
who drifted down the Amstel
with their women and their nets
two thousand years ago.

Their villages still float
bridged to the ancient shore,
but they have addresses now,
tiled roofs and curtained windows.

They work in brokeries and breweries,
computer agencies and fashion marts.
They shop in supermarkets
and communicate by email.

The life of waters calls them still
across the meadowed banks,
but in the long process of time
they have forgotten how to fish.

## Windmills

With only a quiet slap of canvas,
the small domestic gesture
of flapping table cloths,
the great arms make their cycle.

Their quatrefoil adagio
dances against dipping clouds
as though the two were locked
in unseen choreography.

The mill has waltzed with wind
and rain down the arched floor
of time, lifting thatched skirts
to shoo the centuries away.

## Van Gogh Museum, Amsterdam

Should we climb up on our knees
as pilgrims do at Guadalupe,
threading stairs with throngs of tourists,
the whine of electronic guides
singing in our ears?

He no longer frightens us;
they have him safe in frames here.
Mothers no longer point him out
to warn their children away,
but present them to his paintings
like an audience with the Pope.

We have tucked him safely in the past
and fear no strange assaults
upon our eyes.  His venerated works
belie the madness of his mind.
Throngs wind in hypnotic strands
paying their postmortem penance
for his lifetime of neglect.

## The Raising of Lazarus
## by van Gogh

How reluctantly Lazarus stirs
from eternal sleep, his ghostly form
slowly reassembling.  Insistently
the green prophet gestures,
yellow sun his shimmering halo.
The sprouting earth, the heavenly flame
force life upon the limp figure
crumpled in the shadowy cave.
Mary kneels, inert with fear,
not knowing how the fierce contest
will end, or if she still wants
what God was asked to give.

# GERMANY

## On the Rhine River

There is nothing wild here;
all is washed in human presence,
all tailored by human toil.

Someone was here before us,
pressed his pattern to the earth,
laid his vision brick by brick.

It is not ours to change,
to pull down and start again,
but only to restore and purify.

We are not adventurers but keepers
of old stones to be reused,
old vines to be regrafted.

We take our mothers' places
in the same neat rooms,
the same white walls and window boxes.

We have conserved, maintained,
swept the house and settled in
to claim we've made a life.

## Cologne Cathedral

Here one feels the load of time,
the compressed presence of our kind.
I understand the mystery
of why the restless young would flee
the fate of always fitting in,
knowing even where our skins
would lie in death, the certainty
a cipher has in formulae.
I know now why the brave escape,
how kin define but suffocate.

## Hard Hat Zone

The world expected concrete,
steel, the clear glass face
that mimes its anonymity.
Erase time's traces. Forget the old
empire and start again new
and fashionably minted,
was the crass demand
of the conquering alliance.
But Germans refused that order
and built the old world back.
Each golden leaf of plaster gilt,
every colored floweret
of every lacy stencil
was faithfully applied
to every reconstructed wall.
With each loving brush stroke,
every precisely restored cobblestone,
their message became clearer:
it was not the culture that failed;
it was the fools that failed the culture.

## St. Jacobus Church, Rudesheim

There is something real here,
something that resists the flux of time,
that will not bend to fashion craze
or auction off its history.

The city is a wily shopkeeper
with trinkets rattling in each hand,
a smiling wench with golden teeth
and beer upon her breath.

But here within this stony fortress,
back-to-the-wall with Commerce, Inc.,
we hear above the hawkers' cries
Bach's stately *Passacaglia in C.*

## Gutenberg Museum, Mainz

Reflect upon the unexpected role
of metal bits reshaped to letters,
a co-opted wine press,
and doghide ink pads.

Think how an idle student's game
of scrambled alphabet
was played in dusty corners
among wood chips and metal flakes.

Picture the fume-filled print shop
thundering with heavy presses,
busy apprentices in spare moments
assembling the Western mind.

## The Residenz, Wurzburg

The world divides
into those who reign
and those who are reigned on.

## St. Stephen's Dom, Passau

We await the organ concert
with the cherubs who make ready
for their flight, the prophets
who strain against the pilasters,
the golden saints who supervise
the pulpit, and the altar angels
who sail their mythic vision
into the paradise aloft.

This plaster company stares down
with pity and contempt
upon our gawking human swarm
shifting noisily on wooden chairs.
We are tending calluses,
flashing cameras and pointing
in astonishment at the airy
domain floating high above
while waiting for the concert.

## Monastery at Melk

One cannot die for lack of beauty,
so they say, though something
pertinently human fades away.
Nothing marks beauty's absence
like the sunken sockets
of the starving or the flushed brows
of the fever stricken.
Fantasy does not attain
the rank of bread and water,
nor does religious ecstasy
substitute for sanitation;
which is why the vote would go
to chipping all the gold from Melk
and spreading it thinly
across the hovels of South Asia.

## Danube in the Mist

The Nibelungen must have lived
in depths like these,
climes indistinct, mysterious,
down thick white currents flowing
upon the slate-gray water.
In this blind world, sound
is sextant, magnet, compass.
Voices rising from the banks
seek human mooring.  Boat horns
warn unseen travelers through the fog.
Anything could take shape
and rise from the blinding spume:
dragons breathing fire or fish-tailed
maidens luring sailors to the rocks.

## Vacation Houses, Nuremberg

The land calls to us,
summons us from sterile offices,
from glowing terminals,
tellers' cages and robotic factories.
The land beckons, and we go
as best we can to rented cabins,
minus our familiar comforts,
set on plots like postage stamps.
We go to turn the soil and smell
its fecund breath, to plunge our hands
into the mystery of root and rock,
the dark domain of worms.
We come to strip away evasion,
to reach into the heart of things
down to where good and evil simplify
into flower and weed.

# AUSTRIA

## Schonbrunn Castle, Vienna

Not the mirrored hall
with a thousand candles lit,
or the dining room heaped
with porcelain and crystal,
nor the French bedroom bordered
in gold leaf and Gobelins —
nothing seems significant
beyond the incidental fact
that in this unimpressive room
Mozart lifted childhood hands
to play the royal clavier.

# HUNGARY

## Kalocsa, Hungary

The sad musicians of the Czardas
go remotely through their paces,
gypsy music swirling, howling
from their flashing hands.
Nothing moves across their stony
faces as they play these duty pieces,
rhythms that move tourists
down rows of merchandise,
melodies that wheedle money
from their ample pockets.
Music leaps from the musicians' fingers,
but nothing sings within their souls.

# TURKEY

## Hillside Scene, Trabzon

Queen Anne's Lace grows waist-deep
beneath a pair of gap-toothed
Turkish crones, mirror-posed
like the inverted queens
on the death card of a perished world.
Silhouettes upon the cement barrens,
they veil their aged eyes
against the ever-changing dawns.
Anatolian sibyls, their ears alone
hear the forlorn cry from the ghosts
of Hittite horsemen racing
through the streaming tides
of a million smokestacks.

## Tour Guide

He has it down to art now:
the pregnant pause at cliff-edge,
the outflung arms, the pose,
voice lilting in oration.

He points to a spit of land
where his grandmother was born,
thus assuring us his presence
is mirror to this patch of earth.

He whisks our open lorry
to the British side of roads,
horn blasting toward a hairpin
curve to secure our passage.

He quotes a range of rental prices,
lists accommodations visible
above the radiator, conjures
visions of exotic indigestibles.

Clearly he wants us back: our crazy
language, pointless questions,
frequent calls for bathroom stops,
but most especially, our money.

## Cemetery at Aya Sophia

Stones tilt against walled stones
in the garden of Aya Sophia
where turbaned dead effendis
stand immortalized in stone.
An angel with bent wings
and face worn featureless
climbs a spire of Arabic.
Ranks and files of Greek,
tall thin legions of Latin
proclaim the venerable histories
of those whom time has swallowed.
Even the proud barber
displays in death
his marble brush and scissors.

## Istanbul by Bus

We straggle in as camel trains once did,
out of the dust and heat of lonely
caravanserais, loaded with rugs,
tea glasses, tiles, fabric, silver,
collective gleanings from the tourist trade.
We see the city glistening by early light
with a strange sense of recognition.
Istanbul: where the East ends
and the West roars in.

## Monastic Cells at Zelve

Here it is easy to mortify the flesh.
The unrelenting sun is adequate itself
to stun desire and defoliate dark urges.
Here God wears the face of wilderness
where men once shriveled to bare souls
strung along the cliffs like desiccated
mushrooms.  Here God is praised
by silent psalms of rock, blue litanies
of sky, and canticles of bright space.

## Motel in Çanakkale

One of those worn places where the drain
hangs motionless as Dante's cold empyrean,
where man and fly have reached a state
of easy toleration.
Clean by dint of women's sweat,
quiet from a flagging tourist trade,
its doors sigh open to a trickle of termite dust.
Its sheets smell of wind and the lye soap
that shrivels hands.
The floor, cement cool, repels the fading sun,
offering austere solidity to refugees
from the tumble of frost-pocked roads.
It is as it is, pretending to nothing more,
but it will do to hold tomorrow
in dark abeyance.

## Urn Burial, Antalya Museum

After death the slight body
was washed and folded like fine linen,
knees tucked beneath the chin,
robe snug about the feet.
The hair was braided, hung with beads,
swirled into a simple crown.
In the hands are spoons, fish hooks,
a bag of seeds, a clay pipe.
Nothing needful is left to chance.
No provision is omitted.
From the beginning they knew
we are not without destinations.

## In Pamukkale

At the pools one sees our species bare
without the subtle nuances of scales or fur,
more like slugs stranded on a dry day;
pale sausages, perhaps, some miscue
of the butcher's craft.
Seeing them forked over silted ledges,
mantis-legged, broiling like cave salamanders
under July sun, one senses little kinship
with their noble effigies ensconced
upon the fountain ledges at Perge.

# AFRICA

## Village in Togo

It is still there:
music unprocessed,
uncommercialized,
raw and right.
It still emerges from human fiber
directly over human tongues,
unamplified, unadorned,
as lived.
Its patterns are simple,
its details intricate,
feet and drums its rhythm
conveying the local mind
in dialogues of sound.
Form and content are trim, precise
like the seamless circles of women
swaying to the bright bands
of woven tone.

## Village Fire

I struggle to imagine their worries,
these mirrors of my sex, moving
burdened about the village fire.
These same gestures
cooking, washing, cradling
are utterly my own.
Their thoughts are more elusive,
holding me at a distance
with wonder or contempt.
The inobvious emotions
held deep beyond us all,
are curved, folded, looped
among our waiting persons
into a place completely shared,
completely unaware.

# Bushman-speak

Your tongue and mine
inhabit different worlds,
yours exponentially complex,
a langscape where verbs
crackle in the mouth,
your tongue zigzagging
between clucks and hisses,
exclamatory kisses
hanging ripe on noun trees.

My langland is worn
clear down to plains
spouting dull pronouncements
in bare, efficient sayways,
your fierce ruts and ditches
smothered in grammatical
asphalt. When we talk
your langway ends in singing,
mine in dictionaries.

# TANZANIA

## At Olduvai Gorge, Tanzania

This is as close
as we can come
to home,
as close as sense
can take us
toward our source,
as close as mind
can bring us to the distant
shores of memory.

In the vast scar
bleeding down through Africa
time tears earth to bone,
to shards of skull whose blank
sockets stare out bluntly
with a human gaze.

Here among the anthropoid
remains we yearn to recognize
the first green fistula protruding
from the simian tree, the chromosomal
twig that burst into a branch.

Time has left no trace of memory.
Not a flicker of recall
betrays the link.
No faint remembrance here
of ancient earth
stirs in our primal brains,
only an intuition
that in such broken places
we might find ourselves.

# NIGERIA

## Lagos, Nigeria

Hustle, or you die!
To live is to sell, to buy, to bargain,
returning by dusk
through anonymous alleys
with something to eat, to wear, to trade.
Lagos: a town become a frenzy,
a mercantile insanity
distorting farmers into tradesmen,
feet into wheels.
More motors, more horns,
more moving, more contending.
One must choose
in this place without pity
to sell
to beg
or to die.

# IVORY COAST

## Museum at Abidjan

Like the small fountain
overflowing the pebbled walk,
spilling green cress into weltered herbage,
the glyptic images overflow the walls,
pressing down upon us the burdened thoughts
and sensed impulses of the gathered past.

The closely huddled ancestors jostle,
tribe against tribe, fecundity,
spirituality in ritual celebration.
The collective concerns of homo sapiens
lean from these plaster walls,
turn in slow fan currents,
settling heavily on damp summer air.

# Encounter

Only an eyeblink separates him
from the Nigerian forest
where he stands in leaves and feathers,
come to rescue us from the blind world
of machines and convey us to the spirits.

His ancient kin searched out the way
to the far edge of oblivion
where he comes to take us
by the voice of rattles, the flicker of fire,
the smoke of flesh burning on his altar.

He is the lord of chant and dance,
master of rhyme and ritual
conjuring up that grand dimension
distant as falcon flight,
permanent as wheeling stars.

We sit transfixed while he weaves
muscle and bone, color and movement
into a swirling knot of power
that tightens to a coil, plunging him
into an ecstatic trance.

We expect dead souls to visit,
springs to burst from stones,
trees to whisper with their leafy voices,
but we have been too long away.
The spirits do not remember us.

We are not healed, not enlightened.
The delusions of our power go undissolved.
We merely sit like guilty boulders
looking sheepishly across the fire
at the exhausted shaman.

## Customs Declaration

One ceramic bowl: $5.00
      (It was the color of silver,
      retaining my finger print
      as though summoning my hand.)
One wooden bowl: $6.50
      (The inside smelled as though
      just shaped, raw and round
      from a rib of tree.)
One green dress: $7.00
      (In which to dream of Senegal
      and the Wolof women
      floating through the markets
      like French aristocracy.)
Two yards of cloth: $5.50
      (Meant to grace a hip
      or sling a sleeping baby
      to some maternal back;
      destined for a transformation
      to a tablecloth.)

## Pan American 092

We are floaters, roots hanging,
yanked stubbed and bloody
from the packed soil of habit.
We are transitors stuck midway
between histories, caught
in shifting landscapes
of collective memory.
We are prospects in a scheme
of meticulous invention triggered
at gate 17 and rolling forward
like unexposed film
on a five week reel.

# TIBET

## Aku Tonpa

Trickery twirls on turns of phrase,
misplaced inflections, slight
omissions, cross-identities.

While the landlord doled out wheat
on loan and chortled
at the profit he would make,

Aku Tonpa counted on
a slight of tongue to extricate
the loanees from their indebted state.

When the dreaded day
rolled 'round, he shuffled
fundless, to the landlord's house.

He danced with uncouth vigor
on the latter's stoop,
after which Tonpa proclaimed

the debt was paid in full,
the word for "wheat" and "dance"
being, in Tibet, the same.

# The Snow Lion

One does not see snow lions.
No guided tours exist to point
them out. No endangered species
act protects their frail existence.

Snow lions are a frame of thought,
a construct of the wakened mind,
an incident of consciousness
when nothing special is expected.

Only after meditation, years
of shedding dailiness, days
spent unshackling time, hours
passed chucking objectivity

into some vast oblivion
does one occasionally intuit
a white form separated slightly
from the snowy anesthesia.

The truly gifted may retain
the state just long enough to catch
its crimson grin, that secret smile
with which the universe began.

## Mandala Offering

The tall monk inhales slowly, his red robe swelling
like a sun-struck cloud.  From somewhere
near the bottom of the world a tone arises,
sizzling like loose gravel down our ears' curled
cochlea.  Sound without tune or time
hangs its dense crimson curtain
over our transfixed heads.

From the delicate webwork of overtones
that shimmer the vibrating air a pure soprano
chord erupts like sprays of yellow light.
The strange nimbus dances on a stream
of steady breath.  When the long phrase shivers
to its wispy end, the elusive female
vanishes into mystery.

# The Dance of the Five Dakinis

These spirits have ascended,
in their lumbrous, elephantine way,
to heaven, chuckling their drums
like elevated laughter.

They cannot shed their peasant past,
but stomp their feet against the earth
as though to reassure themselves
this solid world is real.

Dakinis come to beckon us
to higher ways, to emptiness of mind,
but so full-bodied is their dance
as to betray their errand.

So they twirl and rattle,
sashes swaying, feet thumping,
telling us despite themselves
that heaven is joy at hand.

## Purification

Delusions, 84,000 they say,
but whoever counted so high?
What paranoia would parse every act,
every thought into such calumny?

Thinking of them creates subtler minds
to help us awake from our sleep,
so they say, but I wonder if error so large
doesn't suffer from estimate creep.

One gentle monk lifts his watering pot,
a bouquet of feathers attached.
He pours to a gold ceremonial bowl
to help all our sins come unlatched.

Gliding about in their mystical space,
the monks chant each flaw by its name.
They banish our blindness with watery slosh.
We should leave not so dense as we came.

## Laying Stones

It is always here to there:
the white jet paths
that spiderweb the skies,

Interstate 95 that glows
like friction tape
under vapor lights,

or these cement stones
that wobble in their cradles
no matter how I dig them.

If I were Buddhist,
here would be enough
to fully occupy my mind,

but I am an American
with foot itch, one wild
continent lurking in my genes.

I must have a there
to get to, something smacking
of a destination

that immediately becomes
a here, which is why I go on
laying stepping stones.

# JAPAN

## On Yamamoto Street

Morning breaks with a slam of shutters,
and the chatter of street pavers
slurping miso soup and green tea
by the curb where evening rain
sizzles in the sunlight.

Already Sugo's folded futons decorate
her house wall, bowed respectfully
to those next door.  Mainichi Daily
reports a giant sale at Seibu and the fall
of Shoji's real estate empire.
The water is off again.

Yamato-san, late come and overhung,
is not awake. His wife is frazzled.
Hosogawa's dog, in a standoff
with the postman, growls deeply
and bristles at the gate.
The water is off again.

So this is the world I've wakened to,
dazed from a twelve hour flight,
but certain that even in this guise
I'll find the same human inventory.

## Reluctant Journey

Think of all the money spent
moving bodies, flinging flesh
across date lines and climate zones.

Think of all the time wasted
relocating this or that
pile of protoplasm here to there.

Corpuscles feel no urgency
to be up and going.
Ask any cell; it will demur.

The fault lies with the brain
that stalls if not transported
frequently for profit or diversion.

The rest of us can putter happily
around the house while the brain
is busy plotting its escape.

The body may groan and protest,
but once the brain barks its command,
arms and legs fall into line.

# SOUTH AMERICA

## Amazon Camp, Peru

Rain on thatch
is not like rain
on tin, wood, shingle
or any human thing.

It strikes gently,
laving the pleated channels,
glistening at the fiber ends.

Rain opens sky to earth
in quiet dialogue,
at light's end
a shower before sleep.

# MEXICO

## Altun Ha, Yucatan

The archeologists fling blue tents
over the limestone cliffs of Temple A.
The tap of their hammers, the swish
of sieving fills the grassy plaza.
They pull up tree roots, reset stones,
and catalogue common artifacts.
Their sweat falls into the wash tubs.
Their bandaged fingers grasp the trowels.
Nothing they find will give them wealth.
Nothing they learn will bring them fame.
Yet they stay, unable to believe
a thousand Mayan years
meant nothing after all.

# At Torrero's Restaurant

Thumpa, thumpa, wheeze

Diners chew rhythmically
on the beat of a bass guitar
washing down the pepper sauce
with hot licks of accordion.

Thumpa, thump

Jaws cracking crisp tostados,
Pico de gallo, sizzling tacos.

Ai, yi, yi croon the cancionistos
to a booth of office girls
with mouths like chili pods,
their feet dancing flamenco
with chair legs.

Thumpa, thumpa

Trays steam by, dimpling
the air at every pulse;
cold beer and hot tamales,
flan and enchiladas.

YEEEEEEEHA! Thumpa, thump

# UNITED STATES

## Key West, Florida

The kooks, the skags,
the geeks, the fags,
the distinctly uncool
fled to this coral frontier.

They festered here among
the conches, the fishers
and the spongers
who offered surly tolerance.

It was an uncombed,
unzipped bed-on-the-beach
cast of misfits that spawned
a cult of informality.

"So picturesque," the realtors purred
as they divied up the land,
raising the ante on each hovel
to some Manhattan level.

The middle class invaded
bringing condos, supermarkets,
theme restaurants, cruise ships,
children marched from K through 12.

You look hard now to find
the wastrels getting a buzz on
under a scraggly banyan
wreathed in marijuana fumes.

They are pushed to the edges
of the tourist trade
in a city safe and sanitized
that doesn't want them any more.

# Mallory Square, Key West

It isn't Stonehenge
where the ancients chanted
hymns to the dying sun.

It is a sea of bare arms waving
to the thump of steel drums
skittering on alcoholic air.

There are no torches meant
to light the frosty earth
and conjure back the sun.

There are the fire eater
and the trick cats leaping
through a flaming hoop.

No hunched masses quiver,
fearful of the coming darkness,
knowing time might end.

These unruly celebrants
hoist their Margaritas and cheer
the dying of the light.

The ancients erected stones,
somber testaments to the mystery
that contained their lives.

This mob leaves a pile
of beer cans and vaporous butts
of questionable cigarettes.

## Hubbing in Atlanta

"Bora Bora" proclaims a purple shirt.
"Yale" another modestly intones
in black. "I Talk Surf" shout
the red cotton backs of passing hunks.
It is Main Street world, a frieze
of passing dialects quick-frozen
to the walls. It is Shuffle City,
a bipedal panoply of thongs and laces,
a strap and buckle bourrée
to the whine of gate announcements.
Here creatures of the air temporarily
alight in restless chair pods
clinging to aisle edges.
Their feeding stations glitter
to a neon rhapsody:
"World's Best Yogurt" winking
rhythmically to the "Hot Dog Special".
Ice cup maracas rattle over plastic
counters, playing sidemen to a squeal
of restroom doors. This is Nowhereville,
Rootless-on-the-Tarmac, and we are
earnest catechumens in the ritual
of flight. "Boarding now at Gate B,"
rasps the station agent.
"Fort Sumter" brags the blue coat
disappearing down the hall.

## Durham, North Carolina

## Sunday at Duke University Chapel

Somewhere in the growl and rumble of bass pipes,
somewhere wedged between the howl of Mixtures,
somewhere among the stone reverberations of the nave,
somewhere in the congregation's wobbling vibrato
is the tune to this damned hymn.

**Boston, Massachusettes**

## Crossing Massachusetts Ave. at M.I.T.

"Walk" the light says, and we do,
across the steaming asphalt swimming with paper,
pen tops, old subway tokens, the detritus of life
in dusty laboratories and those temporary shelters
students designate as home.

For this instant we are captives in a momentary flux,
fragments of all the human passages
that have shaped this rippled plain.
A vast turbulence of memory roils the tar.
We have stirred the unseen universe of dreams,
vague purposes that float above the surface.

"Don't walk" the light says, and we hurry
toward the curb, having left our small indent
on the vast, undetectable realm of human striving
that wafts unceasingly above the street.

# Minneapolis, Minnesota

## University of Minnesota Library

The white spaces roll like foamy breakers
through the driftwood stacks.  No bird cries here.
The low shell hum of Xerox
permeates this marble cave.
I have been down to P88 feeding on the sea bed,
plucking papers and the inky leavings
of some published octopi.  I am in borrowed
ocean; the robed effigy of the scholar-founder,
his oiled splendor theatrically lit,
inspects my voyage from mid-cascade of stairs.
The small stemmed eyes of Lumina blink
their monitors like iridescent creatures
of the deep.  I touch their keys and stare
at the kaleidoscope of text, the bright display
my chart and compass in this sea of print.
I steer for mooring toward the Reading Room
where cotton jackets float like sails
across the chairs.  Beyond, the great dock
Circulation verifies my manifest.
I off-load through the Exit dinghy
to the sunlit shore.

# Middlebrook Hall, University of Minnesota

Brown — the color of old clay pits
and dusty brickyards somewhere down the Mississippi.
Styled punchcard anonymous with inscrutable facades
of poker players. A twelve floor aviary
on the human flyways between continents;
credo to the temporary state.
We are roosted in this pinwheel nest between
the ancient river, the tall glass pyramids
of pharaonic businessmen,
and a relic of migrated faith.
Summer lazes by our window, a video of changing weather.
Shadows circumnavigate the streets oozing with the steam
of rain vaporizing up the walls.
Rooms shine now with scraps of sun seeping
downward through the lindens, wind-scented
with their soft white powder
sifted out upon the dusk.

## Mount Rushmore, South Dakota

Smug,
that's the expression,
the superior detachment
of those who've passed beyond
the fears and worries of the tourists
swarming there below
in presidential tee shirts.
With a ten thousand year guarantee,
one can afford to sport
a bored indifference
to the mortal world
of sweat and scratch.

## The Badlands, South Dakota

Filaments of cottonwood blow like sails
across the lakes of grass as they did
before mendacity and greed dyed the earth
blood red.  Men died fast then
from bullet or arrow, and women slowly
from malnutrition and despair.
Now, cattle barons and the farmers
they burned out find equal place
beneath the plains. The Indian
equal desolation.  The innocent sky
and blameless hills still undulate
toward the horizon, keeping time
with the universe.

## Jackson Hole, Wyoming

On one side, the barren crests
share first name privilege with clouds.
Gray slabs jutting from the prairie floor
keep their frosty mien while others shed
to summer garb.  They are the avant garde
of force, the legions of kinetic thrust,
belt buckles of the continent.

On the other side, round hills welcome armies
of pole pines. Cows and skiers graze the slopes.
They are the sentinels of wear, bearers
of the tedium of service, stations on winged
flyways, the paths of wolf and elk,
wearing human habitation as jauntily as caps.

## Devil's Tower, Wyoming

Slim stone pillars
disappear in mist.
All that remains
are voices of climbers,
a soft antiphony circling
the gray forest
of fallen monoliths.

## Shoshone National Forest, Wyoming

And on the third day
God created wilderness
without the Wall Street Journal,
tacos, genuine Indian moccasins
from Korea, Coca-Cola,
cigarette butts, theme tee shirts,
or cute names for rock formations.
No queues, Minit Marts,
billboards, neonscapes,
amplified music, rodeo ads,
revivalists, disposable diapers,
bottle tops, U-Hauls, or thong sandals.
God surveyed all that had
been omitted and
God pronounced it good.

## Shell Canyon  Falls, Wyoming

The maidenhair fern that grows lustily
on ascending ledges, drinking great gulps
of crystal air is not aware
(nor should it be)
that its smorgasbord is churned from white
water cascading through sixty million
years of canyon.

## Yellowstone Park

Irrefutable proof
that wilderness and tourists
do not mix.

## In the Rockies

We have no business here.
Such places, sacred to themselves,
must be inviolate.
Mankind should come
on tiptoe, carrying away
such elements as time
can easily redeem.
We have no Berlitz guide
to read these semiotics
of raw power.
Our ears are far too brief
to catch these vast syllables
stretched like rock umbrellas
over countless eons.
Let us go now,
pulling the green curtain
of the unknowable
down between us.

# Twilight, The Grand Canyon

The sun has made final passage
through a thousand tourist photos.
Far below, in the blue veils
drawn across the Colorado,
hikers munch granola
and curse their avocation.
Shuttle buses have disgorged
centipedes of human legs
to ramble Hopi Point.
Electronically wired Japanese,
dangling over the cliffs,
are recording the last rays.
Beyond sight in a muffled roar
the mountains are expiring
in a fit of laughter.

# How We Came to the Canyon
(an imaginary history of the Navaho)

Out of the white song, under the shadow
of the dawn mountain we passed one day
into the warm earth's wrinkled hand.
Our feet touched her furrowed flesh
like raindrops drumming to the rhythms
of our hearts.  We did not know the chants
of this new place.  We could not understand
the whispers of the cedars or eagle cries.
The great creases in Earth Mother's hand
frowned like stony thunderclouds.
Far above, a columned cliff face arched
into a smile, its lips trembling with people.
Their houses clustered like swallows' nests.
Yellow carpets ringed those lofty places,
their fragile threads waving in the wind.
An ancient man came from the mountain
ledges to pick a golden tuft.
He stroked it gently, spreading it like jewels
about our feet.  "Corn," the old one said.
The turquoise mountain sang. The abalone
mountain laughed aloud. The silent sun
pointed a shimmering arm far down the earth's
cupped palm, making water sparkle
through the rocks.  Evening Star shot his silver
arrows down to mark the place.  Wolf Spirit
howled a distant welcome, and we knew
that we were home.

# An Eight-Sided Life

You always know where you are
in a Hogan.
There is little doubt about your proper place
in the universe.
The door always faces Dawn
so you can come in new each time,
leaving the hurts and burdens
of the world outside.
One side faces South so you will not forget
your barefoot childhood and become
an aging grump.
One faces North so you can bear
the battering of life's storms,
having all the rest to lean on.
One side always faces West to remind you
that none of us is permanent.
The other four sides verify that nothing
ever comes without connections.

## Tsaile, Arizona

Not seen straight on but only in that peripheral
brown study astronomers reserve for distant galaxies.
Not quite there, having escaped the small
dignity of mention on the Triple A road map.
Tsaile, simply felt like the tingle of a pink electric
field spread across a sunrise.  Little more
than a sudden elevation and a gasp of wonder
as the prairie falls away to shadows.
Found only by feet following the corkscrew trails
of sidewinders, the delicate nail prints of horned toads.

Having found me long before I searched for it,
the place regards me now with the half-averted gaze
dogs use when they want us to believe
we are ignored.  Tsaile lets me stand, a suppliant
in the scrub brush, vectors of dry heat searing
my bare legs, while it thinks me over.
The empty desert poses my novitiate koan:
what does one hope to find in an absent place?

# Canyon de Muerte, Arizona

How nothing ever vanishes completely:
the waves of some lost river
still there in the crests and ripples
of its sandy bed.
How universal pain is:
three hundred  Navaho
mercilessly starving
on an isolated rock.
How strong our urge for permanence:
a thousand years
of petroglyphs insisting,
"we were here."
How deep our instinct for identity:
countless outlined
hands proclaiming
their particularity.
How brief a time we share:
here between these red rock
walls, tomorrow already
touching yesterday.

# Old Roads

The Appian Way
goes limping off
through the scrub campagna,
a stubbled remnant
of imperial glory.

Forlorn U.S. 90 lopes
by fits and starts
between town squares
and farmers' markets,
ghosts of closed motels
rattling on its shoulders.

All the wagon roads
that never made it into asphalt
disappear in dusty clouds
or wet, potholed conclusions.

Ferry trails that poled
across the gray Ohio River
each sank to watery oblivion
under an iron bridge.

The world is pockmarked
by these souvenirs of false
starts and random disconnections,
places closed or vanished
where the engines of change
roared through.

## Geysers

The white steam plumes are warning flares,
danger signals of the earth's vile temper
barely hidden below green crust
and the blue glitter of lakes.
Here are the cracks in its facade
where sociable demeanor falls away.
Underneath we see the molten rage
that fires the universe.

## Bear Lake, Utah

We  stand above an aqua slice,
208 feet deep and three states wide.
Below bright beads of cars string down curls
of asphalt where Mormon wagons struggled
across the slopes.  Our tourist buses clinging
to this scenic overlook, mayflies
in the scheme of time, to be flicked off
the mountain's edge by the idle thumb of fate,
rolling us like marbles down the trails.

## Kachina

Its maker points to his signature with pride.
"The Wolf," he states, flashing the bug-eyed creature
draped in rabbit fur before my captivated gaze.
Sixty bucks seems modest for this snarling effigy,
resplendent in its beads and feathers.
"It is your guardian," he hints, stroking the silky
pelt as though to rouse the fetish.
Its red eyes stare into dead cornfields
past the hulks of rusting cars and mounds of empty
beer cans.  It could not protect this dying world.
Perhaps it will have better luck with mine.

## In the Cascade Mountains

Earth melts from top down like rock fondue
in glacial dip.  Mt. Rainier's white volcanic
bowl blossoms to the sky.  Clouds scoop out
its glistening gift, showering snow
across its igneous brim.  Drifts fray to water
like white balls of yarn wiggling down the cliffs.
Far away it trickles cold and clear
from someone's kitchen tap.

## "Just Pies"

the mountain cafe sign announces to the road.
Tour buses ch..ch..chuffle up the loose rocks
defining a brief yard, brakes sighing,
doors flung out, disintegrating into people.
Lunch queues straggle up the board porch,
waving wasps buzzing out the ripples
of the tin roof, reading on the shaggy wall
the luscious inventory:  Bumble berry,
Saskatoon Berry thick as tundra,
indigo as distant lakes.  Apple filling melted
amber oozing under pastry cliffs that crumble
beneath our forks.  Rhubarb red as sunset,
thinned to rosy pools at saucer's edge.
Topping all, a dollop of whipped cream
leaking like a glacier into sugar islands.

## Snow Tunnels

It is the weight, the pressing presence of black earth
grinding down upon the ceilings.
It is the sudden fear of raw insistence rushing
at the walls that lifts the follicles across the neck.
Passing down these bright intestines, one speaks
carefully, avoiding reference to the dread
that hangs invisibly in this artificial air.
The smallest tremor of the great Mother
shivering in her sleep, and we are doomed.

# CANADA

## Banff, Alberta

We are processed like hot sausages,
extruded from tour buses,
packaged into meal and cruise agendas,
plied with plastic totem poles, mink key chains,
and bear logo tee shirts.
We are cooked in hotel saunas and refrigerated
in Sulphur Mountain cable cars.
The Hudson Bay Trading Company lives on.
There's plenty of hootch for foreign Indians
roaring in on the Canadian Pacific.
Listen to Chief Kicking Horse, who knew
the merchants with the junk jade
always have the upper hand.

# Grouse Mountain Cable Car, Vancouver, BC

The red gondola settles on the light
thatched patchwork of Vancouver
like a bird ruffling down upon its nest.
Blue dusk fluffs around the sun-lined mountain,
fingering steel cables whistling through the air.
Like the night work of invisible arachnids
the great web spins to and fro
slowly knitting sky to trees.

# Victoria, British Columbia

Streets seethe with restless adolescents,
green haired hop-heads scratching up a buzz.
Their legs make hop-scotch hatches
down the sidewalks.
"Spare some change," they grin
through chin stubble and alley grime.
They are the legions of the strayed,
lost, thrown away disciples
of the temporary state, living by the hard
rock rhythms of the groin.
They copulate on the brick steps
of Immaculate Conception.
Achieving malnutrition in the waste bins
of MacDonalds. Taking essential hygiene
in the fonts of public parks.
Without tomorrow, stripped of yesterday,
feasting like drugged buzzards
on the sensate ruins of today.

# ALASKA

## Portage Glacier

Here ice and rock are locked in deadly combat,
the cold blue plane scraping relentlessly
at the black stubborn stone.
This ruthless contest has absorbed ten thousand years
of wasteful strife.  The glacier frays in sheer
exhaustion, breaking off at ocean's edge
into icebergs white as floating corpses.
The mountains heave out of the struggle,
scarred and rounded featureless
by the senseless feud.

## Express Train, Denali

We wobble north, trampling
the gray skirts of silted rivers,
rolling wheel-deep in fern beds
flared with fire weed.
Mist dots the glass dome
of the observation car, reflecting
alders marching up the hills
to protest our passage.

A scattering of cabins settles
sparsely through the cedars,
their raked paths attached
like umbilical cords to the train tracks.
A fragile human presence is marginally
sustained by this locomotive lifeline,
the only mortal remedy for hunger,
darkness, and the terrible alone.

## The Wilderness, Denali

We are barely here,
and nothing here
wants our token presence.

The caribou tolerate us
as they do June flies,
their clustered pestilence.

There is nothing here we want
to aid our comfort or longevity,
nothing to provide convenience.

We must come here purely,
taking only what it gives:
encounter with the wholly other.

# Denali to Fairbanks, Alaska

We are in the far,
the space on space
of the barely perceptible.

We rest in an eternity
of land and sky,
one disappearing to the other.

We are caught in length
and breadth, the frozen
poetry of the barely mobile.

We are held by the slim hope
that somewhere rises out of nowhere
at the paling of the light.

## Fairbanks to Beaver Creek

I shall drown in this immensity,
gurgle my last in this ocean
of space rolling out from snow
peaked perimeters into green bowls
of prairie grass and fire weed.

It contains me, tightly clamped
to utter lassitude, helpless
while the miles roll out
ceaseless parades of stunted spruce
and duplicated files of willows.

This land is only here because
it glues Alaska to the Yukon,
a million miles of up and down,
a dreariness of sideways
slipping into nowhere.

## Kluane Lake

The snow-cracked mountains
do not care, nor does the water
offer its reflection for my eyes.

The mirrored clouds are not concerned,
and scrawny trees that cling
to permafrost do not respond.

I have no power to affect,
to shock, to please, no need
to act with due concern.

Here is pure freedom, uninvolvement
like these living things. Strange
how freedom feels like loneliness.

## Saxman Village, Ketchikan

Consider this small case of symbiosis:
Anglo-European hordes pouring
from the cruise ships to clamor
over the domesticated ruins
of the old earth cultures.
Indian entertainers offer
the sentimental trappings
of an extinguished cult.
See how they live in sufferance,
in a stark, uneasy barter
of facsimile for sensation,
a theater of parasite and host.

# At Sixty Below in Prudhoe Bay

Breath freezes on expulsion, tinkling to boardwalks
in a rain of slivered ice. Words shrivel on the tongue,
frayed to scrollends flapping curvatures of air.
Wind claws under woolens, painting exposed skin
the gray color of death.
White on white prevails in these minimalist wilds
where figures pass dimensionless
upon unfeatured wastes. Cold, encelled and cancerous,
eats in bleak efficiency through bark and fur.
Days pass to black on black, vanishing like chimney
smoke down the blank hole of night.

Another age would summon gods to the circled
dance of fire. Another time would offer chants
and magic runes against the dark.
Another people heard the beat of Raven Spirit's
onyx wings rippling across the gale,
the gray wolf's ghost howling moons
to ride the frozen land.
Bear masks grinning through the flames
evoked the sun and promised green,
conjuring the blooming tundra
in the pools of children's eyes.

Now Oilmen ride the pipeline trails
in pickup trucks and curse the snow.
In noisy bars the fellowship of mutual discomfort
rails against stale beer and scarce women.
Their transient ears hear nothing more
than the promise of quick cash and a ticket home.
The vast cycle wheeling between earth and ice
is merely inconvenient.

# WASHINGTON

## Pike Street Market, Seattle

Monk fish displayed on chipped ice glaciers,
their fixed eyes staring with glassy accusation.

Sweet peas rivaling the spectrum, bobbing
over clay pots like a friendly neighbor at the fence.

Crabs in lotus posture, fat pink claws clamped
against their carapaces, stacked twelve deep
like knobby prayer wheels.

## Mount St. Helens, Washington

Like visiting day at the cemetery we trail in,
a curious entourage clamoring with kids
and dogs, our campers lumbering
around the curves.
We pick our way among charred sticks
that once made tall green totems
up the mountainside.
We speak with reverence here, remembering
that recently in the sizzling whoosh
of one gaseous belch the leveled landscape
blanched gray and seared to this bleak desert.

# Going

Rocks hardly move at all
but rest calmly where the earth
decides to place them, thinking
long expansive rock-thoughts
that take eons to coalesce.

Trees seem mostly satisfied
with small branch journeys
in and out of space, graceful
bendings for the wind to comb
their needles, and slow folding
beneath the weight of snow.

Turtles in my urban pond
are glad to savor varied densities
of mud, the changing scene of edibles,
the shifting vesture of the water,
all within a few square yards.

Perhaps I've no excuse for being
thirty thousand feet in air,
bound to see moose and glaciers
that will not note my presence,
but seeds are like that, birds in season,
and even fragile butterflies.

What calls us out beyond our roots
to places often inhospitable?
Are we plain bored silly,
or do we sense some urgency
as deep and sweet as home?

## ABOUT THE AUTHOR

Sharon Scholl holds a doctorate in Music and Humanities from Florida State University. She is designated Professor Emeritus from Jacksonville University (FL). She has held fellowships from the National Endowment for the Humanities, the Woodrow Wilson Foundation, and a Fullbright Fellowship to Turkey.

Under a grant from the Witter Bynner Foundation for Poetry she produced a six part TV series on local poetry venues and personalities.

She is the author of *Music and Culture* (Holt, Rinehart & Winston) and *Death and the Humanities* (Bucknell University Press). Her individual poems have appeared in such literary reviews as Oasis, Kalliope, Northwoods, and Poetry Motel. *Unauthorized Biographies* (Closet Books) is her first poetry collection. She lives in Atlantic Beach, FL.